Thomas S. Kirkbride

Code of Rules and Regulations for the Government of Those Employed

in the care of the patients of the Pennsylvania Hospital for the Insane, at

Philadelphia

Thomas S. Kirkbride

Code of Rules and Regulations for the Government of Those Employed
in the care of the patients of the Pennsylvania Hospital for the Insane, at Philadelphia

ISBN/EAN: 9783337373344

Printed in Europe, USA, Canada, Australia, Japan

Cover: Foto ©Suzi / pixelio.de

More available books at **www.hansebooks.com**

CODE

OF

RULES AND REGULATIONS

FOR THE

GOVERNMENT OF THOSE EMPLOYED IN THE CARE OF THE PATIENTS

OF THE

PENNSYLVANIA HOSPITAL FOR THE INSANE,

AT PHILADELPHIA.

BY

THOMAS S. KIRKBRIDE, M.D.,
PHYSICIAN IN CHIEF AND SUPERINTENDENT.

·

THIRD EDITION.

PREPARED AND PRINTED BY AUTHORITY OF THE BOARD OF MANAGERS.

PHILADELPHIA:
COLLINS, PRINTER, 705 JAYNE STREET.
1878.

CONTENTS.

INTRODUCTORY REMARKS.

THE history of the institution for which this code of rules an l regulations has been prepared, extends back to the year 1751, when a number of the benevolent citizens of Philadelphia founded in that city, the Pennsylvania Hospital, which, besides its admirable provision for the indigent sick, is distinguished as being the first establishment for the care and treatment of the insane, in America.

With the exception of a short period immediately after the foundation of the institution, till the first day of 1841, the insane were received and treated in one wing of the original hospital at Eighth and Pine Streets; but its position in the midst of a flourishing metropolis, its contracted buildings, its limited extent of ground, its want of privacy, and, above all, its having no distinct medical organization for the department for the insane, rendered it obvious that a different arrangement, with a more rural location, would have many important advantages.

Fortunately, the wise foresight of the early managers of the hospital had secured a number of vacant lots around their original structure, and the

2

sale of these, in 1836 and 1837, produced a fund from which a farm was purchased, and the buildings now known as "THE DEPARTMENT FOR FEMALES" OF " THE PENNSYLVANIA HOSPITAL FOR THE INSANE," were erected, and furnished for the accommodation of patients.

Between 1856 and 1859, a new hospital was erected on the grounds of the Pennsylvania Hospital for the Insane, and this new structure, in the latter year, was occupied by patients, and is now called " THE DEPARTMENT FOR MALES." These last buildings were provided entirely from private contributions. Two additional wings, at the Department for Females, put up from a legacy of the late Joseph Fisher, and called " the South and North Fisher Wards," were opened in 1867, and 1874, respectively.

It will thus be seen that the Pennsylvania Hospital for the Insane is really made up of two distinct hospitals, each intended for 250 patients, and one being for males and the other for females ; thus strictly conforming to the size originally recommended by the Association of Hospital Superintendents, and showing, as believed, after eighteen years' experience, the very best mode of providing for 500 patients in one vicinity.

The Pennsylvania Hospital, in all its branches, is strictly a benevolent institution. Founded by the liberality of private citizens, its main dependence has always been upon the contributions of the charitable, and all its funds are sacredly devoted to the relief of the afflicted, and spreading its advantages among those who could not otherwise partake of them. Every increase of its resources enables it to extend its sphere of usefulness in the community. Except in its very early days, it has never asked or received any aid from city, county, or State, and no one connected with it has any pecuniary interest in its success.

Every one, therefore, who engages in any post connected with an institution of this character, should feel bound in honor to fulfil a part of this great trust, and by a faithful performance of duty to aid as far as possible in carrying out the main objects of its benevolent founders, to make it truly a blessing to every afflicted one that enters its doors. a spot where only kindness and genuine sympathy reign, and where all that is possible, is done to mitigate the sufferings of our fellow-beings.

The Pennsylvania Hospital for the Insane was opened for the reception of patients on the first day of 1841, since which 7663 have been received, and 3519 have left, restored to perfect health ; while a large number have returned home, with various degrees of improvement.

The institution has been steadily acquiring a firm hold on the confidence of the friends of the afflicted, and of the community, and every one connected with it is expected so to act in all things. as to prove that this confidence is not misplaced, but that even a higher degree of it will yet be deserved.

The treatment of the insane was formerly but little understood, and it is to be feared that many abuses and cruelties of a revolting nature were practised upon patients by their ignorant and unfeeling attendants, to the lasting injury of the sick, and the deep disgrace of those guilty of participating in them.

Although the prevalent views of that period may have offered some excuse for such proceedings, no such reason can now be tolerated for a moment, for it is almost as clearly demonstrated as is the existence of the sun on a bright noonday, that insanity, in all its forms, various as they are, is a disease of the brain, to which, under certain contingencies, all are liable, and the subjects of which are never to be exposed to a rude remark or a rough act, but who are always to be treated with courtesy, respectful kindness, and sympathy—who are to be aided on all occasions in finding means with which to interest, amuse, or employ themselves, and who are ever to have excuses made for the wayward, irritable, violent, or careless acts and words, which spring from a disease over which they have no control, and which destroys responsibility for their actions.

These are the only views of this disease that can be held by those about the insane that will allow full justice to be done to the patients. All must remember that the engagement to perform duties in an institution for the insane implies an obligation on their part, religiously, and to the best of their abilities, to carry out all rules prepared by the proper authority, in their true spirit, and to submit without a murmur to such acts of patients as spring from their disease. By a uniform course of steady, unwavering attention, gentleness, kindness, and sympathy towards every one under their care, all employed will certainly command the confidence of those directing the institution, will win the gratitude of the afflicted, and, above all, secure the approbation of their own consciences.

As already said, insanity is no respecter of persons; no one can claim an entire exemption from it; and none of us know how soon we, ourselves, or some of our dearest friends, may require the very attentions we are now giving to strangers. Let us ask ourselves, when almost worried out with our charge—when on the point of forgetting that we have to do with those who are not responsible for their actions,—what kind of treatment we would wish for ourselves or our relatives, if similarly afflicted, what steady kindness, what persevering attention, what delicate sympathy under all circumstances—and we shall know what is due to others. Let us never forget that motto, which, above all others, is appropriate in every institution for the insane—" ALL THINGS WHATSOEVER YE WOULD THAT MEN SHOULD DO TO YOU, DO YE EVEN SO TO THEM."

Come what may, the law of kindness must be the governing one in this institution, and all other qualifications will pass as nothing, if the disposition to carry out this law is absent. Those who do not at heart adopt this sentiment are unfit to take charge of the insane, and those who violate this principle are not wanted here; they are unfaithful to their trust, and can never do themselves credit in taking care of such patients, nor aid in promoting the prosperity of this institution.

It will almost invariably be found that, where we cannot succeed in our object by mild measures, force will fail, and disputes, violence, and recriminations are always productive of injurious effects.

To perform properly the duties of any station connected with the insane, requires high moral feelings, great self-denial, and a severe schooling of the temper and disposition. If this is thoroughly done, every one is enabled to become highly useful in one of the most exalted fields of benevolence. Simply to perform special duties is not all that is required; there must both be felt and shown an active interest in all the patients—a desire to add to their comfort in every way, and to advance their cure, steady efforts to interest or amuse them, a watchful care over their conduct and conversation, and a constant sympathizing intercourse, calculated to win their attachment, and command their respect and confidence.

All situations about the insane are well known to be arduous and responsible, but a faithful performance of duty in any one of them cannot fail to give a kind of character that must prove useful in other walks of life; and it is sincerely hoped that many who may be employed hereafter in this institution, like not a few who have left it, will in after years look back with satisfaction, not only upon the good they have been instrumental in conferring upon their suffering fellow-beings, but upon the direct benefits they have themselves derived from a residence in the institution.

While we are employed here, we must not allow ourselves to forget for a moment, that this noble institution was prepared *for the benefit and happiness of its patients, and not for our convenience or advantage*, and that to promote the former, we must expect many little annoyances, inconveniences, and privations.

The Board of Managers having intrusted to the Physician in Chief the general superintendence and direction of every part of this establishment, he looks forward with confidence from all, for that cheerful obedience to the by-laws and rules, and such zealous and prompt performance of duties at all times, as will add greatly and certainly to the happiness of the patients, and to the reputation and usefulness of the institution.

OFFICERS.

By a reference to the by-laws of the Pennsylvania Hospital for the Insane, it will be seen that the resident officers of the institution consist of the Physician in Chief, Assistant Physicians, Stewards, and Matrons.

By these by-laws, the Physician in Chief is made the official head of the institution, having a general superintendence and control of it, and of all persons employed on the premises; and among his duties is prescribed that of making, with the sanction of the attending managers, such regulations for the government of all engaged in any way about the patients as he may deem proper. The first edition of these rules was prepared before the opening of the hospital, on the first day of 1841, the second in 1850, and the present code, the third edition, is only modified and extended in such respects as experience has shown to be desirable, to secure more fully the grand objects of the institution.

As required by the by-laws, the Assistant Physicians will make regular visits through all the wards, every morning and evening, and at such other times as may be deemed desirable. The morning visit

will be commenced at or near half-past 8 o'clock;
the evening visit will be just before or after tea, or
after the evening entertainment. These visits will
not be omitted under any circumstances. When
one of the assistant physicians is absent, he will
always know that his colleague is to supply his
place.

At all these regular visits, whenever made, the
supervisors will be at hand to accompany the physicians, and the attendants will be at their posts,
prepared to answer all inquiries, and on all such
occasions, they will take care that, as nearly as
possible, every patient is seen, and at the morning
visit—which is a visit of inspection—have every
door opened, that each room may be properly examined.

The same by-laws also give specific directions for
the performance of important duties by the stewards
and matrons, and which are essential to the comfort of the patients. In performing these duties,
they will necessarily come in contact with the attendants and those engaged in the wards, and like
all the other officers, in the performance of their
various duties, will feel bound to know, by frequent
personal inspection, that everything in their department of the institution is properly carried on
—that all persons are faithful to their trusts—and
that the patients are in every way properly treated
and attended to. To do this, they must necessarily
make frequent visits to every part of the house, and
each one engaged in any department will be careful
to receive these visits kindly and respectfully, and
on all occasions attend to the suggestions that may

be made, in a prompt and cheerful manner, as the other officers are expected at all times to report to the Physician in Chief or in Charge, without reserve, the results of their observations.

When the Physician in Chief is absent, he is represented by the Assistant Physicians, who will be applied to in reference to the patients and attendants.

The first Assistant Physician, in Charge at the Department for Males, represents the Physician in Chief, and is to be respected accordingly.

GENERAL RULES.

In making engagements with individuals to take the direct charge of the patients of this institution, it is to be distinctly understood that the hospital contracts for their whole time, and that they are not to leave the premises or their duties, nor engage in work of their own, without express permission from the Physician in Chief or in Charge.

They are expected to perform with cheerfulness, and to the best of their abilities, *all duties* that may be assigned them by the medical officers of the house, and at all times and in all places to do what they can to promote the comfort and happiness of the patients, and the prosperity of the institution. It is hardly necessary to say, that the effort should be made by all persons engaged about a hospital, to see how much they can do for the patients, not how little labor or attention will secure a retention of their places.

They are to treat the patients, every one having business at the institution, and each other, with respect and courtesy. They are to be neat in their dress, avoid careless and slovenly habits at all times, lounging on settees, the use of profane language, all vulgarity, and every kind of act unbecoming their position. As required by the bylaws, and like the officers and patients, they are expected to forego the use of tobacco and intoxicating drinks of every kind while in the employ of the hospital.

When the officers or visitors are present in the wards, the attendants will rise, and be prepared to give such information as may be required of them.

When abroad, all persons are to avoid reporting the conduct, conversation, or names of patients, and are never to speak disrespectfully of the institution or any of its officers, nor visit or correspond with the friends of patients, unless requested to do so by the Physician in Chief or in Charge.

No one belonging solely to the North or South Wing is to go into the other on any pretence, without express leave or in the performance of specific duties.

It is so highly important that patients should, as far as possible, be kept constantly at some pleasant kind of employment—either work of some kind, or riding, walking, or amusements—that no suitable opportunity is ever to be neglected to induce the patients thus to occupy themselves.

While cheerfulness is always desirable in the wards, marked levity of conduct is unbecoming and undesirable among the insane, and all should be careful to make this important distinction.

It is very desirable that patients should leave the institution with pleasant recollections of their stay in it, and every one coming in contact with them can do much to promote this end. Although the testimony of an insane person, of course, is not always to be depended on, and while a few even after recovery seem to labor under some delusion as to what happened during their sickness, still it is undeniable that, in most cases, patients who have recovered are quite competent to give a correct account of what occurred during their sickness, of the treatment they received from those about them, and much other information highly important to those managing hospitals. Although there are exceptions, it is rare, where uniform kindness has been manifested and a genuine sympathy and interest felt in a patient, that an attendant is accused of cruelty or neglect. It is hoped that in all cases this testimony will be such as to increase the standing and respect due to those having the immediate care of the patients in this institution.

The great and never-ending object of all engaged in taking care of the insane should be to give them something to think of besides themselves and their delusions. The thoroughness, the pleasantness, and the persistence with which this is done makes all the difference between efficiency and inefficiency.

It is important that we should have no favorites. While it is not possible to avoid feeling differently in regard to individuals, still it is not proper that our feelings should be allowed to make us different in our manner towards the sick, or our treatment of them. Those who, at times, are most unpleasant and unappreciative of our efforts, are often the very persons who are most ill, most in need of our special attentions, and who will thank us for them, most warmly, when they have recovered.

3

The first impressions of a patient and the friends of a patient, when the former enters an institution for treatment, are often of great importance. It is just here that officers, supervisors, companions, attendants, and whoever may come in contact with them, have an opportunity for showing their *tact*, and giving ideas that will be lasting, and of permanent benefit in the treatment of the case.

When patients have been told by their friends,— as they always must be, before being taken charge of by one of the physicians,— where they are and why they have been brought from home, they must be greeted cordially, and convinced as far as possible, that they are still among friends, have come to the hospital solely on account of their health, and will have everything possible done to promote their happiness and restoration. They should be gradually introduced to those who are to be their associates, and should have shown to them all the attentions that may be pleasant to them. The services of all, and especially of the companions, may be made particularly valuable during the first hours or days of a patient's residence in a hospital.

When those employed have leave of absence, the proper hour for return in the evening, when there is no entertainment, is half-past nine. At a quarter before ten, the gate will be locked, and no person admitted afterwards, without being reported to the proper officer.

All whose duties are specially in the wards, should avoid being in the centre building, unless called there on business.

Courtesy and kindness are to be especially ob-

served between all employed. No matter what the
situation, those who cannot thus act among themselves will hardly have the confidence or respect of
those they are engaged to take care of, nor can they
ever become specially valuable, or secure a high
character in a hospital for the insane.

No one, who has difficulties with another employed in the same ward, or engaged in official visits
to a ward, and so far forgets propriety, as to neglect the courtesy that is due to every one, can be
regarded as at all coming up to the standard required in this institution. Even worse than this is
that defect of character that permits any one, engaged in any position in the care of the insane, to
allow the actions or language of a patient to lead
to a neglect of the usual courtesies to which all have
a right, or the attentions that are at all times to be
expected from those occupying such positions.

Everything like gossiping is to be strictly avoided.
Some otherwise good people seem to be specially
beset with this infirmity. There is no end to the
difficulties and bad feelings which often arise from
this very prevalent disposition to detail the occurrences of one ward in another, or to mention to
others the peculiarities and doings of individual
patients. The rule, therefore, must be imperative
that what is said or done in one ward must not be
reported in another, nor the sayings or doings of
individual patients be made the subject of conversation with others. This caution is specially to be
observed by those whose duties require them to
be in different wards. They must resist what may
be with them a natural inclination, as well as the

efforts of others to draw from them information which they ought to regard as confidential.

No better evidence of unfitness as care-takers of the insane can be given than to find those employed to take charge of them, noticing and resenting the words or actions of patients, passing them by without the usual friendly recognition or salutation, and especially do they expose themselves to the very natural charge of unfitness to supervise the disordered in mind, where they are found quarrelling among themselves, or treating with incivility those who, like themselves, are engaged in a most important work among their afflicted fellow-beings. Everything of the kind must be carefully avoided at all times.

It is now an established rule of the hospital that in both departments, during nine months of the year, on every evening, there shall be some kind of amusement or occupation going on in the lecture-rooms, or elsewhere, in which a large proportion of all the patients shall be able to participate. All employed are expected to take a personal interest in these entertainments, and to do everything in their power to have the patients do so. This applies to the lecture-rooms, the gymnastic halls, and the weekly tea-parties especially. Unless for special reasons, one attendant should always be present with the patients from each ward, and at least a majority of all the companions. Those who are not present should during these hours have a special supervision of the wards, and never leave them without permission.

As this code of rules has been made to promote the welfare of the hospital and its inmates, and the comfort of every one connected with it, it is hoped that violations of them will rarely occur, and that all will feel bound to do what they can to secure obedience to them, and never take offence when their own defects are pointed out or improvements suggested.

3*

DUTIES OF THE SUPERVISORS.

THE supervisors of the respective wings are bound to see that the rules contained in this code are faithfully carried out in every particular; that the attendants perform their duties properly; and that all the patients are made as comfortable at all times, as circumstances will permit.

They will very frequently pass through the different wards, especially those containing excited patients, and occasionally through the pleasure grounds, and will aid and encourage the attendants in their efforts to interest, amuse, and employ the patients in every way in their power.

They will be careful to know that all patients get the full benefit of exercise in the open air, and will see that all who are able to do so, go out walking, as nearly as is possible, for at least two hours, every morning and afternoon.

They will also see that, as far as possible, all patients, when in the wards, who are able, have some kind of occupation, and that the attendants take a proper interest in having them thus engaged, even if there is no special pecuniary value in their employment, as the great object in having patients occupied is to benefit them, not to make a profit from their work.

They will especially attend to the prevention of disturbances among the patients, to the preservation of good order and quiet in the house, to its perfect cleanliness, and in all things assist in carrying out the general views and instructions of the physicians in reference to the treatment of the patients.

They will promptly report all irregularities or improper conduct or unfaithfulness in the performance of duties that come under their notice, will give advice to the attendants, and point out any neglect that they may discover in any of the wards, and once a week will report to the steward all damage done to the house or furniture.

They will always accompany the physicians in their morning and evening visits, see that all the patients are brought under their notice, and, at the former, that the rooms are open for inspection, receive all orders and see that they are promptly carried out. If from any cause they are unable to do this, some of the companions should supply their places.

They will keep a daily journal of their observations, which they will have in the office each morning for inspection by the Physician in Chief or in Charge, previous to the regular visit.

In this journal they will especially note all who are received or discharged, all who are moved from one ward to another, all confined in their rooms, or under any mechanical restraint, and any extraordinary occurrence.

DUTIES OF THE TEACHERS OR COMPANIONS.

THE teachers are expected really to make themselves companions to the patients, to sympathize with them in their troubles and anxieties, and while performing their own particular duties, to aid in the supervision of the wards.

Unless otherwise instructed, they will pass through the different wards frequently in each day, seeing every patient, and looking into every room —especially if a patient is confined therein—unless, as will occasionally be the case, there is some good reason why they should not do so. They will advise the patients in the selection of books, encourage them to engage in the different kinds of employment, suggest means of amusement and occupation, and by their conversation and example do all in their power to promote their happiness, and general harmony, and aid in carrying out the wishes of the physicians.

As may be directed by the physicians, they will impart instruction to certain patients, read, sing, and play for them, superintend the amusements, and occupations in the different wards or workrooms at stated hours, and take such part in the entertainments in the lecture-rooms, gymnastic halls, and at the tea parties, as may be desirable. At least two companions should always be present and take an active interest in these amusements and tea-parties.

The companions are expected, when requested, to take charge of the mechanical work-rooms, the printing, cooking, and whatever else may be done in them for the occupation and amusement of the patients, and they will, on most occasions, be expected to spend a few hours with new patients, in their intercourse with whom, they can do important service in securing their confidence, and giving them pleasant impressions of the hospital, and of those under whose care they have been placed for the restoration of their health.

They will preside at the patients' tables, and be present, as they may be required, when there is difficulty in the giving of baths, food, or medicine.

They are to be especially careful to do everything in their power to make the first impressions of newly arrived patients pleasant, and to cause them to feel that they have come among friends, who will take a real interest in their welfare and happiness.

They will, while in the different wards, carefully observe the general treatment of the patients, and they are to suggest to the attendants whatever they think will add to the comfort of the patients or the tranquillity of the wards, and will report any neglect or improper conduct that may come under their notice.

They will keep a journal of their observations, which they will have in the office, each morning, for inspection by the Physician in Chief or in Charge, previous to the regular morning visit. In this journal they will note, in a general way, the doings of the previous day, what patients they have found locked in their rooms, or under any other special restraint, all wards without attendants in them, or attendants found visiting in other wards, and any striking violation of rules or unusual occurrence that may come under their notice.

These reports of both supervisors and companions are required as much that justice may be done to attendants as to patients, not only that wrong may be detected, but that ample credit should be given for the faithful performance of duties, as well as to refute the unjust charges that are liable to be made by irresponsible or other persons.

DUTIES OF SUPERVISORS OF CLOTHING.

THE Supervisors of Clothing will see that everything of the kind belonging to the patients is examined promptly on its arrival, and a correct register of the same made in the books provided for the purpose.

All clothing received after a patient's admission should go directly to the clothes-room, and there be seen, examined, and registered; and where any articles are not marked, this should be attended to before they are put in use, and especially before they are sent to wash. All jewelry, money, or valuables are to be placed in the care of the steward, who will register the same and have them deposited in the fire-proof.

When patients leave, there should be a comparison between the register list and the clothing sent away, and any deficiencies from loss, wear, or destruction, as far as can be, duly noticed.

Under the inspection of the Supervisors of Clothing, accurate lists of every patient's clothing will be taken, before it is sent to the wash-house, and while one copy of this list is retained in the clothes-room book, another should go with the clothes, and be returned with them after they have passed through the washing and ironing rooms, as by this means it is easy to tell, where any deficiency that may be discovered, must have occurred. Any losses that may be noticed must be promptly investigated.

Whenever and as required, the attendants in each ward are to have the clothing of the different patients properly assorted, in a bath-room or chamber, so that no time may be lost in taking the lists already referred to.

The assorting and distribution of the ironed clothing, bedding, etc., shall be under the direction of the Supervisors of Clothing.

In conjunction with the matrons, and under the direction of the Physician in Chief or in Charge, the Supervisors of Clothing will see to the procuring and making of new and the repairing of old clothing, both by seamstresses and attendants, and also in providing everything of the proper kind, of this description, for the occupation and amusement of the different classes of patients.

DUTIES OF ATTENDANTS.

INTERCOURSE WITH PATIENTS.

In all their intercourse with the patients, the attendants are to treat them with respect and civility, are to address them in a mild and gentle tone of voice, and avoid violence and rudeness of every kind. All nicknames and undue familiarity are to be avoided. All civil questions are to be properly answered. All reasonable requests are to be promptly attended to. They are to keep cool under every provocation; are never to scold, threaten, or dictate authoritatively; but, whenever they desire anything done by a patient, are to make a request in a respectful manner.

Force, unfortunately, has sometimes to be used in every institution for the insane; but tact and kindness render its employment comparatively rare, and whenever it must be resorted to, the manner of using it may be made to take away nearly all its offensiveness. A pleasant smile, a cheerful, kind, and respectful manner, and sympathizing words, will go far to convince even the most excited patients that what is done is from good motives, and that they have little to fear from those around them.

The opposition of patients, and much of their

4

violence, very often arise from delusions that lead
them to suppose that they are to be injured in some
way; and every attempt either to put them in their
rooms, to give food, baths, or medicine, or to do
anything about their persons, if done with angry
looks, cross words, or violence, only tends to con-
firm their false ideas and make their resistance the
more obstinate and determined.

In the care of the insane, few things are of more
importance than patience. Attendants and others
are apt to hurry patients too much in what they
wish them to do. Being quietly seated, a few
moments of patient waiting and gentle coaxing will
often prevent an hour of difficulty and irritation.

The truth of these views is unquestionable, and
is confirmed daily by convalescent patients, who
are able to describe what were their motives and
feelings when highly excited.

Under no circumstances will attendants be excused for striking a blow, or laying violent hands
upon a patient, unless in the clearest case of self-
defence, or to prevent the commission of serious
injury to themselves or others.

Attendants are never to manifest fear of any patients, but, while treating them with firmness and
decision, it must at the same time be with mildness
and kindness.

They must take every proper opportunity to in-
spire the patients with respect for and confidence
in the officers, and to convince them of the true
character of the institution, and of its leading object, the promotion of the restoration and comfort
of its patients.

They are promptly to interfere when patients are disposed to quarrel, and by kind words, and engaging their attention with other objects, prevent difficulty. A kind word fitly spoken will prevent many a scene of excitement, just as a harsh remark, an angry look, an unkind allusion, or a rude act, on the part of an attendant, may be the origin of difficulties which will last for hours.

They are to carefully avoid talking to patients on the subject of their delusions, or to others in the hearing of the patients, and, as much as lies in their power, they should endeavor to prevent others from doing so.

They must never allow patients to be laughed at, ridiculed, or harshly spoken to on account of their delusions or the peculiarities of their behavior. No greater proof of a want of correct feeling could be given than indulging in levity in reference to the afflictions of our fellow-beings.

Deception is always to be avoided, and particular care is to be taken that promises are not made that cannot be performed.

Although there is little restriction in this respect, they should not furnish writing materials or books to the patients, nor make purchases for them, without consulting one of the physicians.

All letters, parcels, or packages to or from patients are to pass through the hands of the physician, or of some one appointed by him. When patients have tobacco, or forbidden articles of any kind, it is the duty of the attendants promptly to report it.

All damage done by patients is to be entered on

a book provided for the purpose, and through the
supervisors delivered to the stewards at the end of
every week.

SUPERVISION OF PATIENTS AND WARDS.

Each attendant is responsible for every patient
under his or her care, and is expected to be able at
any moment to say where each individual can be
found.

Where two or more attendants are in a ward,
they are equally responsible for *all* the patients in
it.   They can, if they choose, divide the work, but
not the responsibility.

If any one is discovered to be missing, report is
to be immediately made to the supervisor and one
of the officers, and the proper search instantly instituted.

An attendant allowing a patient to go out of a
ward is considered responsible for his or her safe
return.

*One attendant must always be present with the
patients in each ward*, unless express directions are
given to the contrary.   When it is necessary to
leave, except for a very temporary purpose, it must
be known that a substitute fills the place.

When patients remain much in their own rooms,
the attendants are to find reasons for frequently
calling to see how they are engaged, or if they require any particular attention.

On certain occasions, one attendant may guard
two contiguous wards for a very short period—but
not otherwise, unless by special direction of one of
the physicians.

MORNING DUTIES.

The attendants will rise punctually at the ringing of the bell, and take charge of their wards before the night watch goes off duty, as it is wished that there should be no moment without some one being responsible for the wards. They will then open the chamber doors, give the patients a kind greeting, at least wish them "good morning," and see that they are properly dressed, well washed, and have their hair and clothes neatly brushed.

Immediately after opening the doors, the attendants will remove the chamber utensils—never without being covered—from the rooms, or have them otherwise properly attended to, and have the bedding laid on chairs for airing. They will then commence putting the rooms and corridors in good order, and, after the beds and bedding have been sufficiently aired, have them properly made up for the day. All this is to be personally attended to by the ward attendants.

Every part of the wings is to be prepared for inspection at the physician's visit, which will be commenced at about half-past eight o'clock every morning.

CLEANLINESS AND VENTILATION OF THE WARDS.

Every part of the wards is to be kept scrupulously neat, clean, and well ventilated at all times.

Whenever any unpleasant effluvium is discovered, the cause of it is to be searched for and promptly removed, day or night.

4*

When any part of a parlor, chamber, or hall is accidentally soiled, it is to be cleaned at once.

Whenever a bed or the furniture of a room has been disarranged, it is to be promptly put in order.

The halls and parlors must be swept as often in each day as is necessary to keep them perfectly clean.

If an attendant from one ward, in passing through another, spills oil, medicine, etc., he or she is bound at once to clean the place.

Unless directions are given to the contrary, the uncarpeted floors of the chambers and corridors are to be scrubbed at least once a week, and as much oftener as may be required.

The spittoons are to be kept clean, and frequently emptied. The water-closets, urinals, etc., are to be carefully watched, and prevented from impairing the purity of the air in the ward.

Nothing is clean enough if it can be made cleaner, and nothing found out of order should be allowed to remain so.

All beds that are soiled are to be removed from the wards immediately after the patients rise in the morning; and after breakfast clean ones are to be substituted. If only wet, the wet straw or hair is to be removed, and boiling water poured through the soiled part, after which it is to be thoroughly dried before being returned to the chamber. All beds and bedsteads are to be thoroughly examined once a week, and oftener, if necessary.

A clean sheet and pillow-case are to be put on each bed at least once a week, and when the spreads become soiled they are to be sent to the wash-house, and clean table-cloths are to be asked for whenever those in use are soiled.

When patients wish to lie down during the day, they are to go to their own rooms for the purpose— and the attendants will see that the bedding is not soiled, and that it is put in order as soon as they get up. The health of many patients requires this indulgence every day, and care is to be taken that it is not improperly refused at any time.

MEALS AND GIVING FOOD.

The attendants will see that the patients are always up and ready for breakfast, at the prescribed hour. They will carefully observe that they pass to and from the tables in good order, returning directly to the wards when they leave the dining-rooms.

When patients take their meals with the officers in the centre buildings, they are to be accompanied thereto, unless they have the full privilege of the grounds.

Those patients who take their meals in their own rooms, or at a table in the ward, are to be served promptly, and especial care is to be taken that their food is brought to them warm, in good order, and neatly served, and, whenever necessary, an attendant is to remain with them while they are eating.

There is no good reason why the patients' tables in every ward should not be just as neatly served, and the food be as warm and as well cooked, as at any other table in the hospital; the hospital has amply provided everything necessary to have all this so. Where it is not so, complaint should be made till it is corrected.

Any difficulty in procuring what is wanted for the wards or the comfort of the patients, and especially on diet orders, is to be promptly reported to the Physician in Chief or in Charge.

Care is to be taken that no knife, fork, or other article that could be used as a weapon, is left in the wards, or taken from the tables. When any such instrument is missed, prompt measures must be taken for its recovery.

The attendants will not leave their wards for the patients' meals, nor for their own, till the ringing of the bell to call them for these purposes. They will return promptly to their wards after finishing their own meals.

The stewards and matrons, as required by the By-laws, will visit, as often as possible, all the dining rooms during the hours for meals, and also have a supervision of the mode in which the patients have their meals served to them in the wards, or in their rooms. These visits will always be courteously received, and all deficiencies or wants are to be at once reported to these officers, who will see that they are promptly corrected, and their instructions on these points are to be strictly attended to.

Patients are not to be forced to take food but in the presence of one of the physicians, a steward or matron, a supervisor or teacher—and never but by the express direction of one of the physicians.

ADMINISTRATION OF MEDICINE.

The trays containing the medicine cups will be called for at the office by such person as may be indicated by the physicians, half an hour before breakfast and dinner, and at $7\frac{1}{2}$ P. M., or, when there is a lecture, immediately after it is ended. The attendants will receive their trays as they are carried through their respective wards, administer the medicine, see that it is all properly taken, wash the cups, and have the trays ready to be sent back by the individual who calls for them when returning to the office. If there has been any difficulty in taking the medicine, the attendants will state the fact to the person carrying the trays, who will make a verbal report to the assistant physician, or a register of it on a book which will be left at the office, on returning thereto.

The utmost gentleness and patience are to be used in giving medicine, and every proper means employed to induce the patient to take it willingly. When it is positively refused, and the physician believes its administration important, either one of the assistant physicians, stewards, or matrons, supervisors, or companions, must be present, before any force can be used.

When the attendants suppose any mistake has occurred in the medicine sent, or when a patient complains of being sick, or having any unusual symptoms, the medicine should be retained in the cup till one of the physicians can be seen upon the subject.

Any striking or unexpected effect in the operation of medicine is to be promptly reported.

When a patient complains of being sick, or is supposed to be so, at any time, the fact should always be reported without delay to one of the physicians.

If anything special occurs at night, prompt notice is to be given to one of the assistant physicians, so that there may be no unnecessary delay in the treatment of the case.

The person carrying the medicine from the office cannot select a substitute, on any occasion, without the consent of one of the physicians.

BATHING.

Unless a special exemption is made by the physicians, every patient will take a *warm bath* once a week, the temperature to be such as is most grateful to the patient. No matter how excited a patient may be, the utmost delicacy and the least possible exposure must be observed in giving baths.

Unless otherwise specially directed, *hot baths*, administered for medical purposes, will be given at a temperature of 98°, as shown by the thermometer, and this temperature is to be kept up by the addition of hot water as may be required. While in these hot baths, the patients are to have a towel, frequently wrung out of cold water, kept constantly on the head. Where it can conveniently be arranged, immediately before retiring to bed is the best hour for giving this kind of bath. When not otherwise directed, and the patients exhibit no weakness, they should remain in this bath thirty minutes. If the patients appear weak, or complain of any unusual symptoms, they should be taken out of the baths, and promptly placed in bed. When these baths are ready for use, a supervisor or companion should be informed, that they may be present. Mustard *foot baths* should be used at as high a temperature as the patient can comfortably bear, and the addition of hot water will occasionally be required to keep up the temperature. Equal care is to be observed that the water is not too hot. It should at least be tested by the hand before it is used. From one to two tablespoonfuls of mustard should be put in each bucket of water. The feet should be kept in the water not less than twenty minutes. These baths should be taken immediately before going to bed. On lecture nights they are to be given after returning from lecture. No one able to attend a lecture should ever be kept from it to take a bath, which should be given afterwards.

SHAVING.

At the department for males, the shaving of patients is to be done by the attendants, or persons employed for the purpose, in each ward, at stated intervals, and patients who desire to be shaved more frequently are to be gratified in this particular. Great care is to be taken that no injury is done with the razors, all of which are to be carefully kept by the attendants. When the physician has allowed a patient to shave himself, an attendant must always be present, and no other patient in the room at the time.

WALKING OUT WITH PATIENTS.

It is desirable that every patient not too feeble, or too sick, should walk out about the grounds at least once in each morning, and once in each afternoon ; and in pleasant weather at least two hours, at a time, should be thus occupied.

Immediately after the physician's morning visit, in all suitable weather, one attendant in each ward should prepare to go out with as many patients as it is proper to take at once,—the other attendant remaining to do the work of the ward. Upon the return of the first company, a second should go out, and so on till all in the ward have had the proper amount of exercise. In the afternoon, the same plan should be adopted and continued till near tea-time.

When walking out with patients, the attendants will as far as possible consult their wishes, in regard to the direction of the walk, allow them to rest, when desirous of doing so, visit the summer houses, museums, and amusement halls, and take every means to make the time pass pleasantly. They should be vigilant to keep them together and prevent their strolling,—take care that those from different wards mix as little as possible, and that no more are taken in one company than can be properly attended to.

When patients' habits are careless, the attendants will see that they do not lie on the ground, or improperly expose themselves to the sun, etc.

Attendants, when out with patients, will avoid entering into conversation with each other, reading, etc., by which their proper supervision may be prevented.

These walks in the open air are as much for the benefit of the attendants as the patients, and should never have the appearance of being a hurried task, to be finished as soon as possible.

No patient can remain out after tea in summer, nor after sunset in winter, without special permission from one of the physicians.

All patients going out to walk beyond the yards must be accompanied by an attendant, unless the physician has given them the privilege of the grounds. Those having this privilege are expected always to be punctual at meals, and in returning to the wards are to avoid entering the centre building or basement story,—unless a special privilege has been granted,—or remaining standing about the gateway, or on the pathway leading from it to the centre.

If any patient, having the privilege of the grounds, or absent by special permission, does not return at the appointed hour, the attendant in charge will report the fact to one of the officers, and ascertain the reason therefor.

Patients are never to be taken upon the *domes* without special permission.

On the Sabbath, patients are not to walk outside of the enclosures, either with or without attendants, except to attend a place of worship.

Only those patients who conduct with entire propriety are to walk in the centre yard, and after $8\frac{1}{2}$ P. M. all employed are to avoid walking there.

New patients are not to be taken outside of the

5

enclosures till the Physician in Chief or in Charge has signified his approbation of their having this privilege.

When attendants wish to take a company outside of the enclosures, they will first report to one of the physicians, whom they propose taking, where they are going, and how long they expect to be absent, and get permission to do so.

When outside with patients, attendants will be especially careful to avoid crowds, railroads, and all other dangerous places. They will strictly avoid paying any visits when they have patients with them, or entering any tavern or house for any purpose.

The Physician in Chief or in Charge alone gives the privilege of the grounds, or permission to patients to pay visits at home or elsewhere.

PATIENTS AT WORK AND OUT-DOOR ATTENDANTS.

Such patients as are deemed suitable will be allowed by the physicians to go out to work, under the care of the out-door attendants, gardener, or farmer; but no one is to be taken out of the wards for this purpose, unless some general permission of the kind has been previously given by one of these officers. The attendants and others will take especial care that the patients do not engage in improper kinds of labor, and that they do not overwork themselves.

These patients must always be kept under observation, and when a strong disposition to escape is manifested, they must be constantly near the attendants.

No patient should be taken out of a ward to work, or for other purposes, by an officer or by any other person, without mentioning the fact to one of the attendants.

All attendants are expected to go out and work *with* patients, whenever it is deemed desirable for them to do so; and when thus engaged, they will carefully avoid every appearance of superintending the patients, instead of working with them, but should induce them to labor by persuasion and example, and not by giving orders to them.

READING IN THE WARDS AND LECTURE-ROOM ENTERTAINMENTS.

Immediately after tea, on the evening of every Sabbath, the patients of the different wards, who are sufficiently calm, will assemble in the lecture rooms in the centre buildings, to listen to the reading of the Holy Scriptures. One attendant from each ward will invariably attend with the patients under his or her care, and who should be properly solicited to be present. When, from any cause, an attendant cannot be spared from a ward, the supervisor will arrange who shall remain in care of the patients.

On each Sabbath one of the teachers of each wing will read portions of the Bible to the patients of the different wards, at which reading one attendant must always be present.

As they may find time, on every day, the com-

panions will read to the patients in the different
parlors or wards. The attendants will take pains
to have all attend who are suitable, and one attendant from each of the wards will always be present.

On the evenings of entertainments or lectures in
the lecture-room, one attendant must be present
from each ward from which patients attend, the
other attendant remaining in the ward to take
charge of it during that period, unless, under certain circumstances, one attendant is left to take
charge of two adjoining wards. But all attendants
not employed in taking charge of the wards are
expected to be present with the patients in the
lecture-rooms or amusement halls.

RETIRING AT NIGHT.

Patients are not to retire before $8\frac{1}{2}$ P. M. without
permission, unless in cases of sickness or fatigue.
After the bell rings at $8\frac{1}{2}$ P. M., or after lectures or
amusements, patients *may* retire in every part of
the house. Those who desire it, may remain up
afterwards, according to their wishes, so that they
retire in time to allow the attendants to close their
doors at a quarter before ten.

Attendants, as well as patients, are expected to
be in their rooms at a quarter before ten o'clock,
and after ten o'clock no light can be kept burning
in any room, unless in case of sickness. In each
ward, however, one light will be kept burning in
the hall all night, to be used in cases of emergen-
cies.

After patients have commenced retiring, all persons are to be careful to avoid making a noise of any kind that might disturb those who are in bed.

In certain wards, as may be directed, the clothing of patients is to be kept outside of the rooms, always neatly folded and placed on a chair or settee near the door, and is to be handed in to the patient when the door is opened in the morning.

Where patients lodge in a different ward from that in which they pass the day, it is the duty of the attendant having them in charge during the day to take them to their rooms and see them comfortably in bed, unless otherwise directed; and it will also be the duty of the attendant of the ward in which they sleep, to see them up and dressed in the morning, and returned in seasonable time to the ward from which they came the previous evening.

Before closing the doors, the attendants should wish the patients a " good night," and be certain that they are actually in their rooms. The doors are then to be locked and tried, to ascertain that the bolts have properly slipped.

Unless there is an attendant sitting up, in or near the room, no patient's door is ever to be left unlocked at night, without special permission from the Physician in Chief or in Charge being given to the attendants of the ward and to the night watch.

SECLUSION OF PATIENTS IN THEIR ROOMS.

Whenever patients become so noisy or so violent that the attendants, after trying all proper means, believe it necessary to place them in private rooms, they should provide assistance such as will convince the patients that resistance will be useless. It must then be done in the most mild and gentle manner possible. When the patients are in the rooms, the attendants should sit down quietly by them, and calmly tell them why they have been placed there, and that they will be released as soon as they are able to control themselves. No matter how unreasonable the patient appears, this should always be done. Under no circumstances can it be justifiable to force a patient into a room, and suddenly close the door, without a word of explanation.

The movable furniture in a room should always be taken out before an excited patient is thus locked in a room.

A room having a wire or close shutter, and, if possible, a wicket door, is always to be selected for the seclusion of an excited patient. As soon as the patient is in the room, the fact is to be stated to one of the physicians, or to a supervisor, or a memorandum of it left on the office slate.

Where it is necessary that patients should be secluded in their own rooms, the attendants should be careful to see to them frequently, to ascertain that they have everything proper that can minister to their comfort, and to know in what manner they are occupied.

When a patient is very violent, one person on each side taking an arm, and a third at the back, can almost always convey any ordinary individual to a room, or remove him or her from ward to ward, with but little difficulty or injury to any one.

RESTRAINING APPARATUS.

The frequent use of restraining apparatus is productive of so many and such serious evils, and is now so nearly abolished in all well-conducted institutions for the insane, that it will not be permitted to be applied here in any case, except by the express direction of the Physician in Chief or the Assistant in Charge, or, in ease of their absence from the premises, by that of one of the other assistant physicians.

Seclusion to a private room, and the personal eare of attendants, must be relied on till a physician ean be found, and his directions in reference to future proceedings given. It is, in most eases, much better for one or two attendants to sit by a patient for some hours than to put on any restraining apparatus, although the latter may, in very rare cases, ultimately be necessary, and even beneficial.

Whenever patients are fastened on their beds by the apparatus used for that purpose, or when their hands are confined in any way, the attendants must never forget that, thus situated, they require constant attention, as they are unable to assist themselves, and may thus easily get into habits that will afterwards give great trouble and annoyance.

ESCAPES.

The escape of patients is always exeeedingly annoying, and, although such events will occasionally occur, it must never be allowed to be from neglect.

Patients are most apt to escape when passing from one part of the building to another, or when allowed to pass out for some particular purpose, or, if near a crowd, or in the streets of a city, or about twilight. At such times and in such places, therefore, they must be particularly watched.

An attendant's eye should always be kept on a patient known to be disposed to escape.

When it is clearly made out that a patient has escaped from the carelessness or neglect of an attendant, the expense of recovering the patient will be charged to the attendant, at the discretion of the physician.

When a patient is found to be missing, a search should at once be instituted where the individual was last seen, and if any traces are discovered, pursuit should be instantly made. But, if not discovered at once, the fact should be promptly communicated to one of the physicians, or other officers or supervisors, and any other attendant that may be met with. The officers will then give directions what course is to be adopted to recover the patient. The attendants following the patient should, if possible, leave word in what direction they propose going, and should know that some one takes special care of the patients they leave. When patients are brought back, no offensive allusion is to be made to the escapes; but they are to be treated in all respects as if nothing of the kind had occurred, except that they are to be watched more carefully in future.

SUICIDAL CASES.

When patients have a disposition to commit injury to their own persons, all experience goes to show that there is no certain security but by constant watching. Care should be taken to place out of reach all the means that would be likely to be resorted to, and the patients must be kept constantly in sight, treated with great kindness and sympathy, and their attention drawn as much as possible from the object. It must never be forgotten that, in a determined case, a single minute of neglect may be as serious in its effects as a whole hour.

Before placing such a patient in a room, it should be carefully inspected; and when the clothing is taken off, it should be examined or removed entirely from the chamber.

Especial care is to be taken of such patients about twilight, or while others are going to or passing from meals, or to or from lectures, and at all times when the general attention is likely to be distracted, as these are the hours when attempts are most likely to be made.

In case an attendant should ever discover that such an accident has occurred, he must maintain his coolness, give prompt relief if any can be rendered, then, if in a room, lock the door, quietly inform one of the physicians or other officers, the supervisor, teacher, or another attendant—but give no alarm that would excite other patients, or do anything that would lead them to discover what has occurred.

DANGEROUS WEAPONS.

Especial care must be taken at all times that patients do not become possessed of knives, razors, pointed scissors, or dangerous weapons of any kind. Frequent search for such articles must be made in the wards, and when the possession of any is suspected, every possible means must be used to discover them.

Anything seen lying about the wards, yards, or grounds that might prove dangerous in the hands of a violent patient, should, at all times, be carefully and promptly removed.

PROHIBITED ARTICLES.

The By-laws forbid the use of tobacco in this institution, so that it is strictly prohibited to patients to use it in any form. In a hospital it becomes a filthy habit, and experience has satisfactorily shown that it is injurious to most persons, and to many excessively so.

Patients are not to have in their possession any razor, knife, or other article that in their own hands or the hands of others might be used as a dangerous weapon.

Patients are not to receive or forward any letters, parcels, or packages of any kind, without the knowledge and approbation of the Physician in Chief or in Charge.

PATIENTS' CLOTHING.

The clothing of every patient is to be examined at the earliest opportunity after admission, to ascertain whether there are knives, weapons of any kind, money, tobacco, or other forbidden articles upon his person. If any are found, they are to be promptly given to the steward for safe keeping.

The clothing of a patient is not to be taken into a ward until it has been examined, and a list of articles taken by the person to whom that duty is assigned. All new clothing sent to a patient should pass through the same hands, and be registered in the same way, before it is used. No unmarked clothes should go to wash, or be used by a patient.

The attendants will carefully see that patients change their clothes regularly, and all reasonable requests in reference to changing clothes are to be gratified.

Soiled clothes are never to be allowed to remain in a patient's room, but are at once to be put among those to be sent to the wash-house. Clothing or bedding very much soiled are to go to the wash-house daily, the others at stated intervals.

The clothing of patients is to be kept neat and clean, and well brushed at all times. If buttons are found to be missing, or holes are seen in a garment, it is to be taken at once to the seamstress to be repaired. If suspenders or other necessary articles in the wards are found wanting, they are to be asked for till they are furnished. Shoes are to be kept tied—stockings gartered—clothing buttoned or fastened, at all hours, and on all patients.

When patients wet their clothing, they are to be changed as often as may be necessary to make them dry and comfortable, even if every hour. The wet part of their clothing may be dipped in hot water and dried, but is not to be returned to the ward without undergoing this process.

Pains are to be taken to induce patients to be neat in their dress, to wear slippers when within doors, and in wet weather to ehange their shoes after walking out.

In the different wings, the female attendants are expeeted, under the instructions of the proper authorities, to take eharge of the patients' elothing, and see that it is earefully preserved and kept in proper order and repair. They will also take charge of any new work, or work to be repaired, that may be sent into the ward, oecupying themselves with it, and eneouraging the patients to give them such aid as will be useful.

Attendants ean do no private work, except putting their own clothes in order, during the hours of duty, without special leave, nor can they employ the patients to do work for them, if there is any required for the house, without the same permission; nor are they to do work for others without the same authority.

Clothing left for patients, or given to them by their friends, must be promptly examined and registered by the supervisor of clothing before being put in use.

VISITING BETWEEN WARDS.

As the duties of each attendant are confined almost exclusively to a single ward, they can have but rare calls in any other unless specially directed by the proper authority to go there.

In going to and from the centre building, they will avoid passing through wards not necessarily in their way.

Patients, too, are not to visit from ward to ward, without permission from one of the physicians— and no patient is to be transferred from one ward to another except by special direction of the Physician in Chief or in Charge, unless some high excitement may induce the assistant physicians to change a patient temporarily.

LEAVE OF ABSENCE.

To those who perform their duties faithfully, it is wished to allow as much relaxation and as much absence from duty as is consistent with the kind of service required, and the welfare of the patients will permit; but, whenever the absence of attendants is deemed likely to be prejudicial to the patients, they are expected to remain at their posts. When wanted in the wards no special time can be claimed or allowed.

Leave of absence is granted only by the Physician in Chief or in Charge. If he is absent more than an entire day, one of the assistant physicians is to be applied to, but not otherwise, except under extreme circumstances.

The usual time for absence will be from $1\frac{1}{2}$ P. M., or after the patients' and attendants' dinner is entirely finished, till the specified hour of return in the evening, except that on lecture or concert evenings, all who may have been out during the afternoon, are expected to return before tea-time.

Promptness in returning at the hour up to which leave of absence was given is always to be carefully observed. If unforeseen circumstances positively

prevent this for any length of time, word should be
sent to the hospital.

Without special permission, no one is to leave the
premises at any time, or for any purpose, unless in
walking with patients. They will be careful always
to be inside the enclosure at half-past nine, and in
their own chambers at a quarter before ten. In
returning to their rooms in the evening, especial care
must be taken to avoid disturbing those who have
retired, either by the noise of walking or loud conversation.

Attendants should not leave their charge during
the day, for any purpose, without the consent of
one of the officers or of a supervisor.

Permission should always be obtained to leave
the ward before going out of it to see any visitor,
and the absence should then be short; and visitors
are never to be taken through the house or grounds
without permission from one of the physicians.

On the Sabbath, leave of absence is always supposed to be for the purpose of attending Divine
worship. If granted for the morning, the attendants are expected to return before dinner; if in the
afternoon (leaving after dinner is fully over, not
before $1\frac{1}{2}$ P. M.), to return by the ordinary hour in
the evening.

In the wards, having three attendants in com-
mon, one will be allowed to go out each Sabbath in
rotation, after breakfast is fairly over—provided
their presence in the ward is not deemed necessary.

When about to leave the premises, the attendants
will call at the office and put their keys on the

hooks or in the boxes provided for the purpose, and report themselves either to one of the physicians, or leave their names and the hour of going out on a slate provided for the purpose, or as may be otherwise directed, and in like manner report themselves on their return.

They are never on any occasion to lend their keys to any person, and especially not to a patient, without directions to that effect from one of the physicians.

When attendants are absent from their duties for any length of time, on their own private business or for pleasure, they will have the loss of time deducted on the settlement of their account, at the discretion of the physician.

Attendants and others employed in the house are not to visit the friends of patients, unless requested to do so by one of the physicians, and they are always to avoid expressing opinions about a case or its treatment.

Attendants, when going out for any protracted absence, should notify a supervisor of their intention to do so.

NOTICE TO LEAVE AND DISCHARGES.

Whenever any employed wish to give up their situations, they are only required to give two weeks' notice of their intentions.

Whenever the institution wishes to dispense with the services of any one employed in the wards, the same notice will be given, or payment made for that

period, at the discretion of the Physician in Chief
or in Charge.

Whenever any one is discharged, however, for
any violation of rules or improper conduct, no such
notice will be given, nor payment made but up to
the time of discharge.

As many very worthy and well-intentioned persons do not possess the natural qualifications to
make them valuable in the care of the insane, the
officers of the institution, in all their engagements
with attendants, expressly reserve the right, at any
time, to dispense with the services of any one by
giving two weeks' notice, or by paying for that
period, and this without assigning their reasons
therefor. It can never be considered as any mark
of disrespect, when individuals are not likely to
gain credit or give satisfaction in a station, to allow
them an opportunity to engage in other pursuits,
better calculated to advance their own interests.

DUTIES OF SPECIAL ATTENDANTS.

SPECIAL attendants are governed by the same rules as other attendants. But, as their duties are commonly lighter than those of the general attendants, they must expect a closer confinement, and a less frequent absence from their charge.

They are to be particularly careful in reference to those under their care—are never to leave them alone unless from special permission, and promptly and courteously attend to their rooms, clothing, etc., and to all reasonable requests that may be made to them, if not inconsistent with the general regulations of the institution.

They are to exercise a general supervision of other patients in the same ward, take a part in keeping it in good order, and at all times, perform such other duties as may be required of them by the proper officers.

DUTIES OF WATCHMEN AND WATCH-WOMEN.

THE watchmen will commence their rounds at half-past nine o'clock, at which hour they will call at the physician's office for directions for the night.

The outdoor watch will keep moving during the night, and give special attention to safety from fire, and to such points as may be indicated.

The indoor watch will keep moving about from ward to ward, during the entire night, and will visit every part of the house at least every hour.

They will know that all employed are in their rooms at the prescribed hour, and, if they have a doubt on the subject, it is their duty to ascertain the fact by opening the individual's chamber door.

They must be kind, gentle, and soothing in their manners to the patients, and take every means in their power to tranquillize those that are excited, and to allay the fears and apprehensions of the timid. They will see that they are promptly supplied with water when it is asked for, and that all their little reasonable wants are attended to. They will be careful to make as little noise as possible in moving about, in opening and shutting doors, and always speak to patients in a low tone of voice.

They will notice particularly all unusual sounds

in the patients' rooms, and ascertain their cause, or give prompt notice to the proper attendants.

When there are sick in the wards, they will pay them frequent visits—attend to all their wants, and if required administer their medicine.

They will always be careful to remove anything offensive as soon as discovered.

They will report to the physicians all irregularities, every instance of neglect, and all violations of rules that may come under their notice in any part of the house, or on the premises—and enter upon the office-book any remarks they may have to make upon the occurrences of the night. They will always report on this book particularly how *new* patients and those who are sick have passed the night.

Should they discover fire in any part of the hospital or out-buildings, if it is not in their power at once to extinguish it, they will immediately give notice to the officers and then to the attendants, but never raise a general alarm.

They are to ring the bells at the prescribed hours, start the fires in the kitchens, and perform such other duties as may be assigned to them.

The attendants being up, and in charge of the wards, at 6 A. M., the duties of the night watchers cease till 1 P. M., after which their time is at the command of the institution till sunset, from which hour they are relieved till $9\frac{1}{2}$ P. M.

THE DUTIES OF THE WATCHWOMEN are confined to the wards occupied by female patients, in which they will spend the night, and be governed by the same rules as the ward watchmen.

All these will be careful to perform their responsible trusts with the strictest fidelity—to be constantly vigilant, and never to sleep while on duty. Any suspicion of a want of fidelity in those employed in night duty, must necessarily disqualify them for their stations. Individuals failing to perform their whole duty, from fear or any other cause, will not be retained in either of these stations. Any failure to report what they know to be wrong, cannot be excused. That full justice may be done to themselves and others, they will be careful at all times to attend to the watch clocks, and never fail to make the proper register.

DUTIES OF THE SEAMSTRESSES.

IF the duty is intrusted to no one else, the seamstresses, under the direction of the matrons, will take charge of the clothing—keep it in good repair—see that it is not unnecessarily mislaid or lost, and that it is properly arranged for use.

They will see that all clothing is marked before it is sent to wash, and whenever they find that articles are missing, they must endeavor to ascertain what has become of them.

Clothing that requires repairs, if more than the attendants can themselves do, should be carried to the clothes-room, each day, by the attendants of the different wards, and the earliest opportunity must be taken to have it put in order and returned to the wards.

All reasonable requests of patients in reference to changes of clothing, etc., are as far as possible to be gratified.

In the wards for females, the seamstresses will attend to the making and repairing of clothes, as may be directed by the proper officers.

They will take especial pains to induce the patients to occupy themselves, and to become interested in their employment.

When required, they will assist in the care of the patients.

DUTIES OF THE MESSENGERS IN CENTRE BUILDING.

THESE messengers will always be prompt in answering the door bell, receive everybody with the utmost courtesy, and having ascertained the object of the call, will see that it is attended to without delay. If the inquiry is in regard to patients, or those having them in care, they should at once find one of the physicians, who will either see the visitor, or say whether the patients can be seen, and where, and what is their condition; and also whether those engaged in their care can leave their wards to see visitors, and for how long a time. One of the physicians will be found, as nearly always as possible, in the general business or physicians' office, and these are the only proper persons to be seen in regard to the condition of patients, the propriety of their being seen, or for giving to attendants leave of temporary absence from duty in their wards. If no one of these officers is at hand, the messenger will lose no time in finding one, so as to prevent any unnecessary detention of visitors or those having business at the institution.

DUTIES OF THE COACHMEN.

THE coachmen will take charge of such vehicles and horses as may be directed by the Physician in Chief or in Charge, and will see that they are always in good order and ready for use.

In all suitable weather, every morning and afternoon, they will drive out with the patients at such hours and for such time, as may be indicated by the physicians, and will be careful that no accident occurs.

They will promptly report any impropriety or accident that may occur during a ride.

They will not stop at any house, nor transact business for any one, while out with the patients, unless they have first received permission or instructions to that effect from the proper officer.

They will avoid all familiarity, or entering into general conversation with either attendants or patients, but will, at all times, answer courteously all proper questions.

The carriages used by the patients inside of the enclosures will be brought up regularly by the coachmen or their assistants, as may be directed by the physicians.

DUTIES OF THE CARPENTERS.

THE carpenters have the immediate care of the carpenter shops, lumber yards, tools, and materials of all kinds belonging to that department of the institution, and are considered responsible for their safety and economical use.

They will not allow any one to make use of the tools or lumber, without the permission of the physician or steward ; and when tools are taken from the shop for any purpose, if not promptly returned, they will report the fact to one of these officers.

They will prevent attendants, patients, or others from remaining in the shop, so as to interfere with the workmen, unless they have themselves been sent there to work.

No materials are to be taken from the shop or yard by any one without permission from one of the officers.

The carpenters will have especial charge of patients allowed to work in the shops, especially when unaccompanied by an attendant.

DUTIES OF THE GARDENERS.

THE gardeners will have the care of the pleasure-grounds, gardens, and green-houses, which, under the instructions of the Physician in Chief or in Charge, they will keep in good order, and will see that all persons who aid in the performance of the work on these parts of the premises do their duty faithfully and in a proper manner.

They will take care of all implements used for these purposes, and see that they are never left lying about the grounds, but are carefully housed and taken charge of.

They are to consult the physicians and stewards in reference to planting, and to the sale of such seeds or plants as may not be required for the purposes of the institution, and keep a correct list of all sales made by them, with the names of the purchasers and the prices attached, which are to be accounted for to the stewards at stated periods.

When wishing to be absent, they will apply to the Physician in Chief or in Charge for permission.

7

DUTIES OF THE GATE-KEEPERS.

THE gate-keepers will remain in or about their lodges, and when they leave them, except for a very temporary purpose, they will see that some persons, selected by the physicians or stewards, supply their places.

They will see that the gates are kept closed, except while some one is passing, and that they are so secured that patients shall not escape thereby; and they will notice particularly that no improper persons enter the enclosure.

They are to be polite and respectful to all persons, visitors and others, who have occasion to pass through the gates, or have business at the hospital.

They are to admit no one, unless on business with one of the officers, before 10 o'clock A. M., after sunset, nor after 1 P. M. on Seventh-day (Saturday), nor at any hour on the Sabbath, without permission from the Physician in Chief or in Charge.

No one, unless visiting one of the officers, will be allowed to remain within the enclosure at night, nor after dark, without express permission from the Physician in Chief or in Charge, and all such cases are to be promptly reported.

They will lock their gates at a quarter before 10 o'clock, previous to which hour all persons should be inside the enclosure. All persons returning after that hour are to be reported to the physicians or stewards, according to their position in the house.

They are to note the hour of going out and returning of those employed in the care of the patients or in the domestic departments.

They will also report each morning to the physicians or stewards the names of any persons employed who may have been out during the night, and the hour of their return.

They are never to ask for a gratuity from any visitor, and they will always refer those asking information about patients to one of the medical officers, and they will be careful about giving information to patients in regard to visitors.

They are to request patients and all others to avoid standing in or about the gateways, and they will be careful to report all irregularities or improprieties of any kind that may come under their notice.

———

ALL PERSONS employed in any way on the premises, and not mentioned specially in these Rules, are expected nevertheless to conform to the general spirit of them in the performance of their various duties.

ADMISSION OF VISITORS.

THE following rules for the admission of visitors, as adopted by the Board of Managers, are appended, that they may be familiar to all employed in the institution, viz.:—

The Board of Managers, recognizing the duty of shielding the insane from all improper exposure, and regarding their right of protection from the gratification of an idle curiosity on the part of strangers just as great while residents of a hospital as in their own dwellings, have adopted the following regulations for the admission of visitors:—

1. Visitors are not to be admitted before 10 o'clock A. M., after sunset, nor on the first day of the week. They are not to be admitted on the afternoon of seventh day (Saturday), unless on special business with the attending managers, or one of the officers of the house.

2. All parts of the hospital not occupied by patients may be shown and explained during the hours for the admission of visitors.

3. No visitor, unless in company with a manager, can be taken into the wards, without permission from the physician to the hospital, or in his absence, from one of the assistant physicians; and when visitors are allowed to enter the wards, they

must always be accompanied by one of these officers, by the steward or matron, or by some person delegated by the physician for the purpose.

4. As this hospital cannot be allowed to become a resort for idle curiosity, it is hoped that the friends of patients, and all others, will carefully avoid prolonging their visits unnecessarily; and those employed in the care of the patients or in the domestic departments are to avoid inviting company to the hospital.

5. The pleasure railroads and other contrivances for the amusement of the patients, are not to be used by visitors; nor are they to enter the museums or pass through the pleasure grounds, except by special permission.

6. It is expressly forbidden to furnish any inmate of this hospital with tobacco in any form; or to deliver to, or receive from a patient, any letter, parcel, or package, without the knowledge and approbation of the physicians.

7. Funds for the use of the patients are to be placed in the hands of the stewards, to be used only under the direction of the physician.

8. Under ordinary circumstances, carriages are not to enter the enclosures. When for any purpose they have been taken to the centre buildings, they are never to be left standing there; and drivers are always expected to remain with their vehicles outside of the gateway.

9. All persons wishing to see patients, or learn their condition, will inquire for one of the physicians.

10. When visitors so far forget what is due to the feelings of the afflicted and their friends as to make

improper remarks to patients, or to institute indelicate inquiries, all persons will be careful to discountenance such a course of conduct, and abstain from mentioning the names of patients, their peculiarities, or any other circumstance respecting them, a general knowledge of which might be painful to any persons connected with them. None of us would be willing to have our own friends, if laboring under insanity, exhibited to strangers, and we are bound in honor, as far as possible, to protect others from a like exposure.

11. No visitors, unless friends of the officers, are to remain inside of the enclosures after dark, without special permission.

CONCLUSION.

THIS code of rules has been prepared, as has been before remarked, for the purpose of enabling all connected with the Pennsylvania Hospital for the Insane to know the principles upon which it is wished it should be managed, and that they may so conduct themselves as most effectually to advance the best interests of the institution, promote the restoration and happiness of its patients, and, it is believed, contribute to their own comfort and satisfaction.

Any doubt in regard to any point connected with the care of the patients, either mentioned or not mentioned in this code of rules, or in any way connected with the care of the patients or the duties of any one, will be cheerfully explained, at all times, by the Physician in Chief or his assistants.

It is hoped that none will ever engage in any of these situations who do not resolve to do all in their power to perform their prescribed duties to the best of their abilities, and who cannot show by their deeds that they have higher motives to actuate them than simply whatever pecuniary compensation it may be in the power of the institution to give them for their services.

It is the wish, too, of the friends of this institution, that those engaged in all of its departments should be of such a character as to have only to know what is right and proper to secure its prompt and cheerful performance. Such individuals are sure to receive, and, what is still better, to deserve the respect and good wishes of the benevolent, and the grateful thanks of those who have been under their care.

To enable all, by frequent reference, to become familiar with the foregoing rules and regulations, each person referred to will be furnished with a copy when entering upon his or her duties. Each attendant's copy is to be sent to the physician's office, with the medicine trays, whenever required, and a memorandum of its having been seen will be made in it by the person to whom that duty is assigned, at stated intervals. It is expected that all engaged in any way in the care of the patients will read these rules carefully, and sufficiently often to make themselves familiar with them, as ignorance of their details cannot be admitted as an excuse for their not being observed.

www.ingramcontent.com/pod-product-compliance
Lightning Source LLC
Chambersburg PA
CBHW020253290326
41930CB00039B/1179